Tin Man Tim

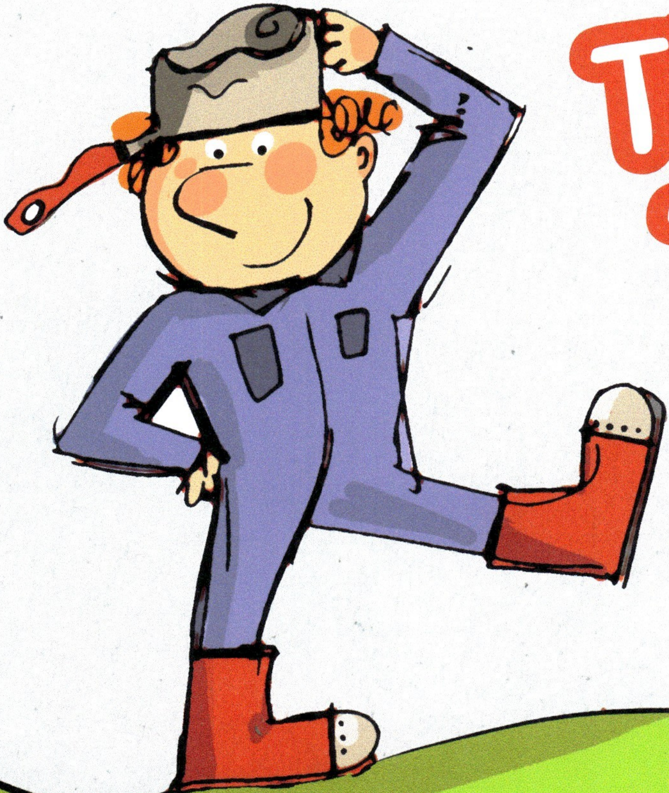

Written by Celia Warren
Illustrated by Giulia Orecchia

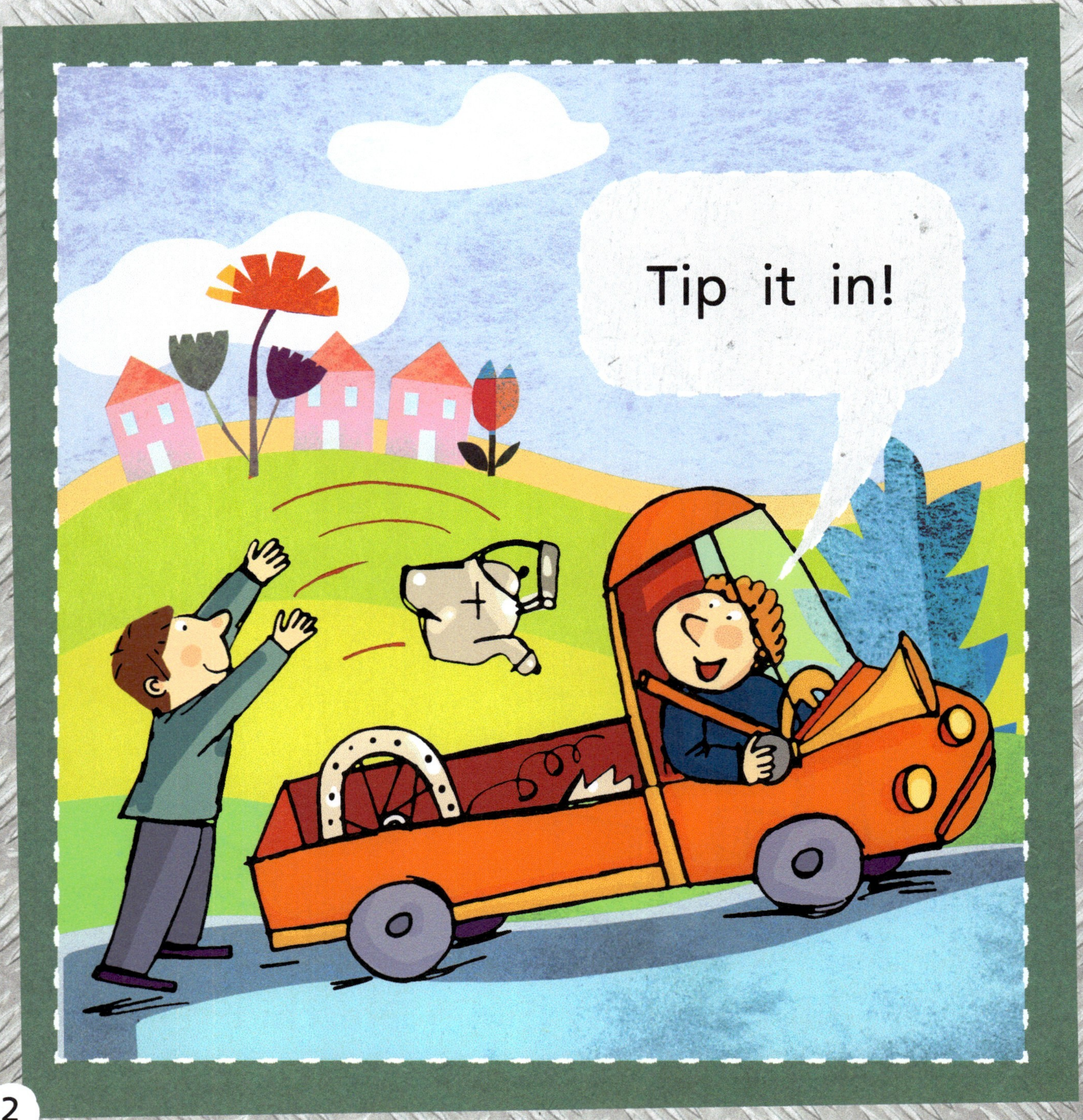
Tip it in!

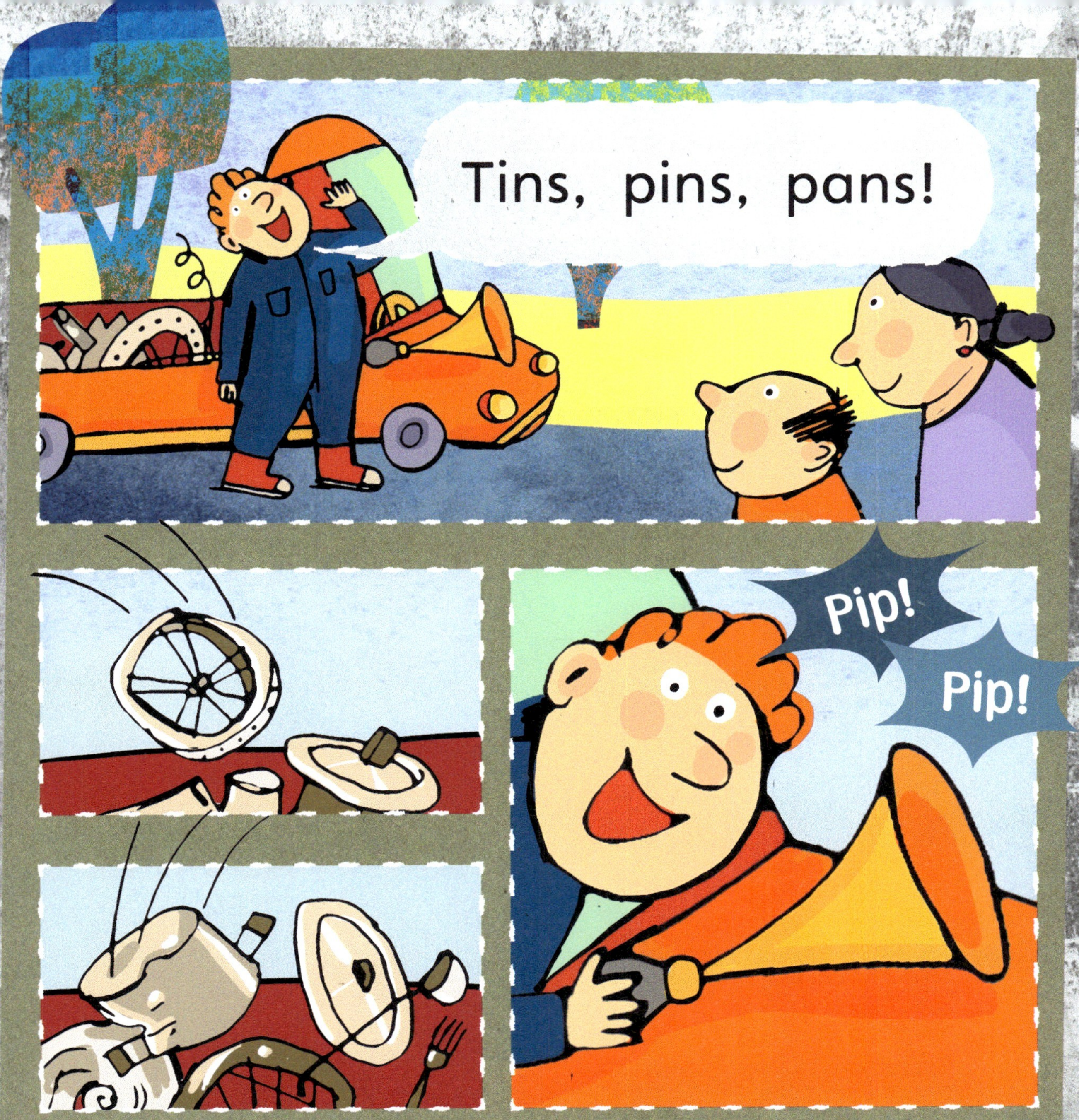
Tins, pins, pans!
Pip!
Pip!

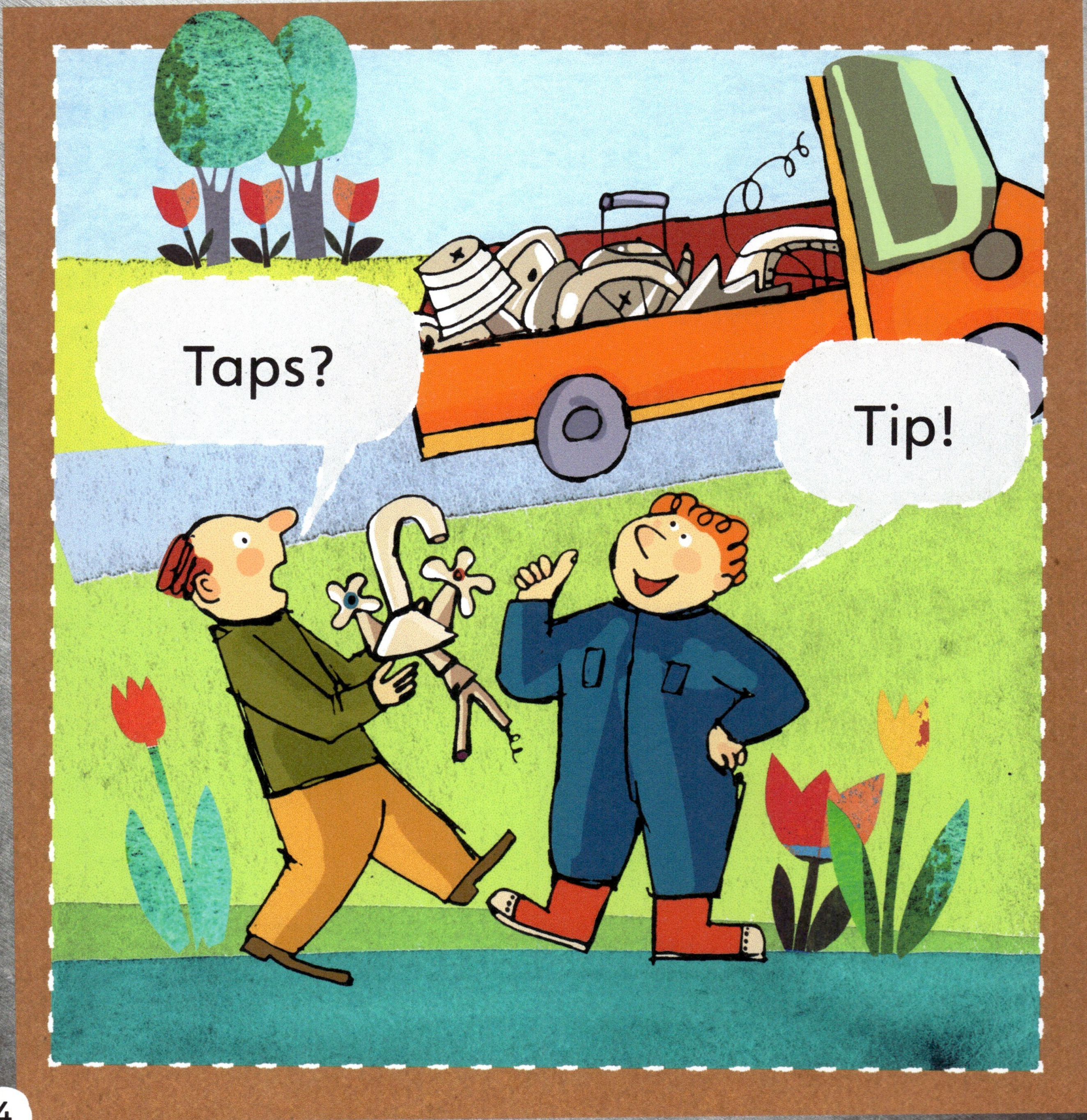
Taps?
Tip!

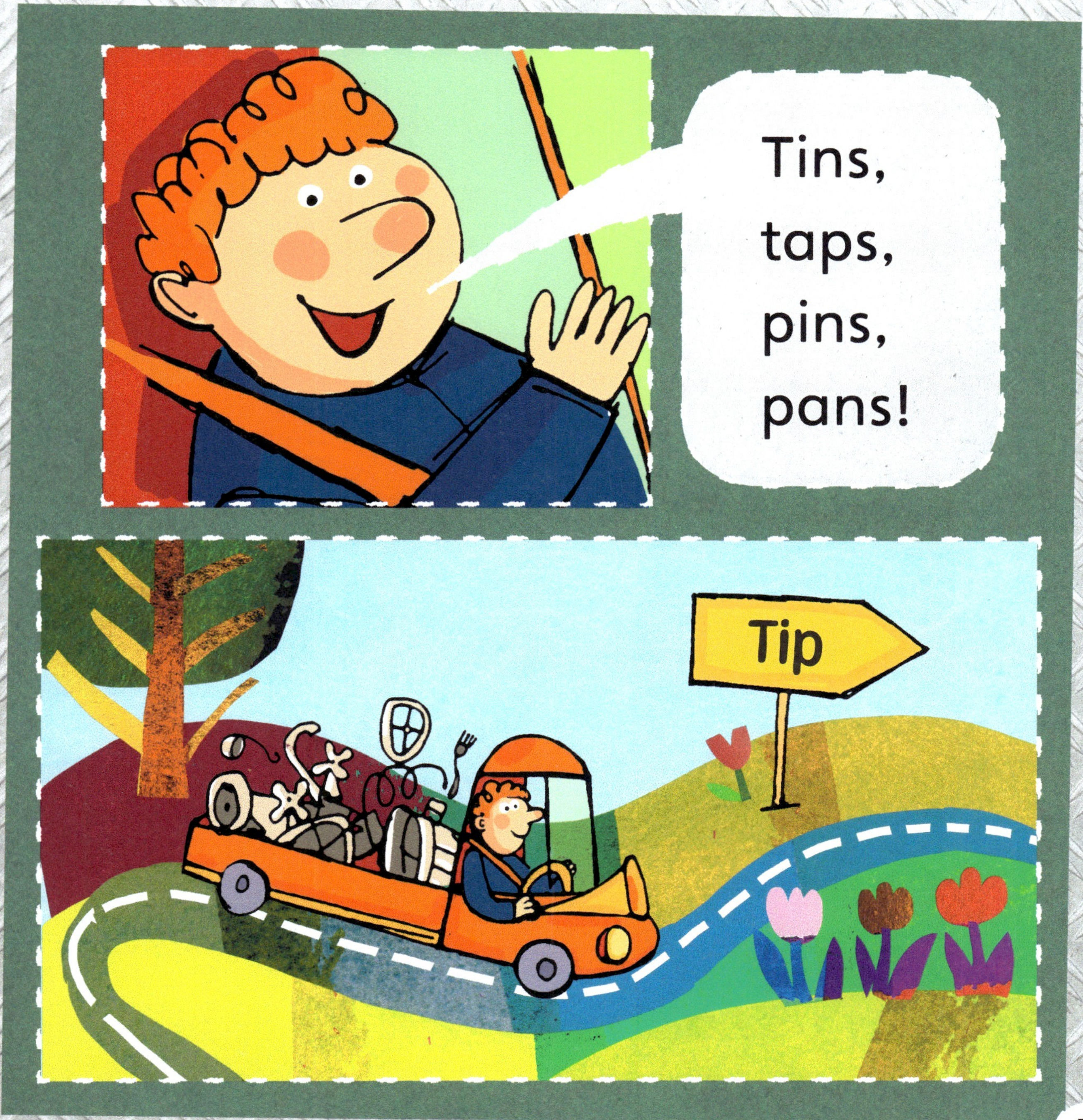
Tins, taps, pins, pans!
Tip

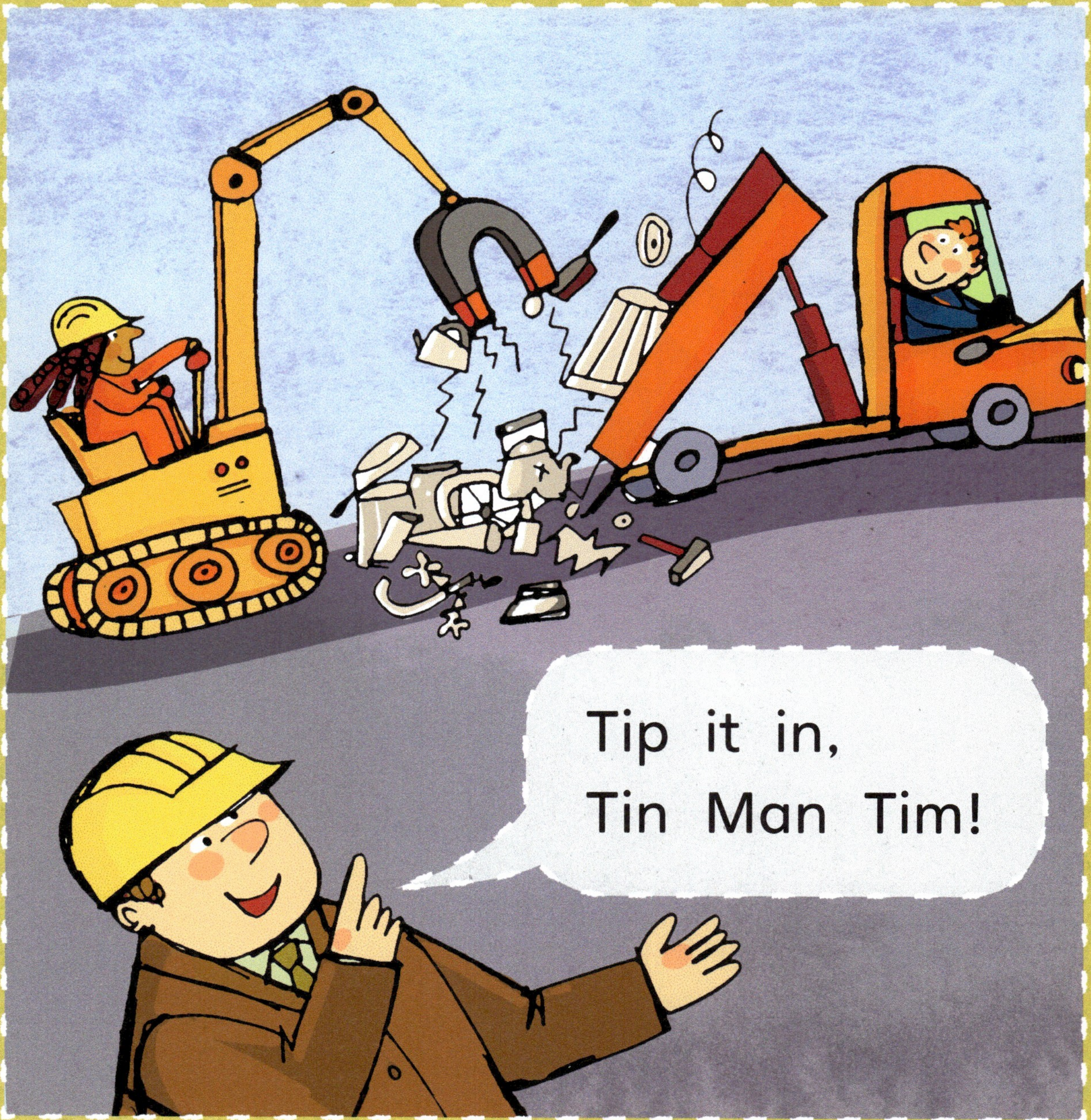
Tip it in,
Tin Man Tim!

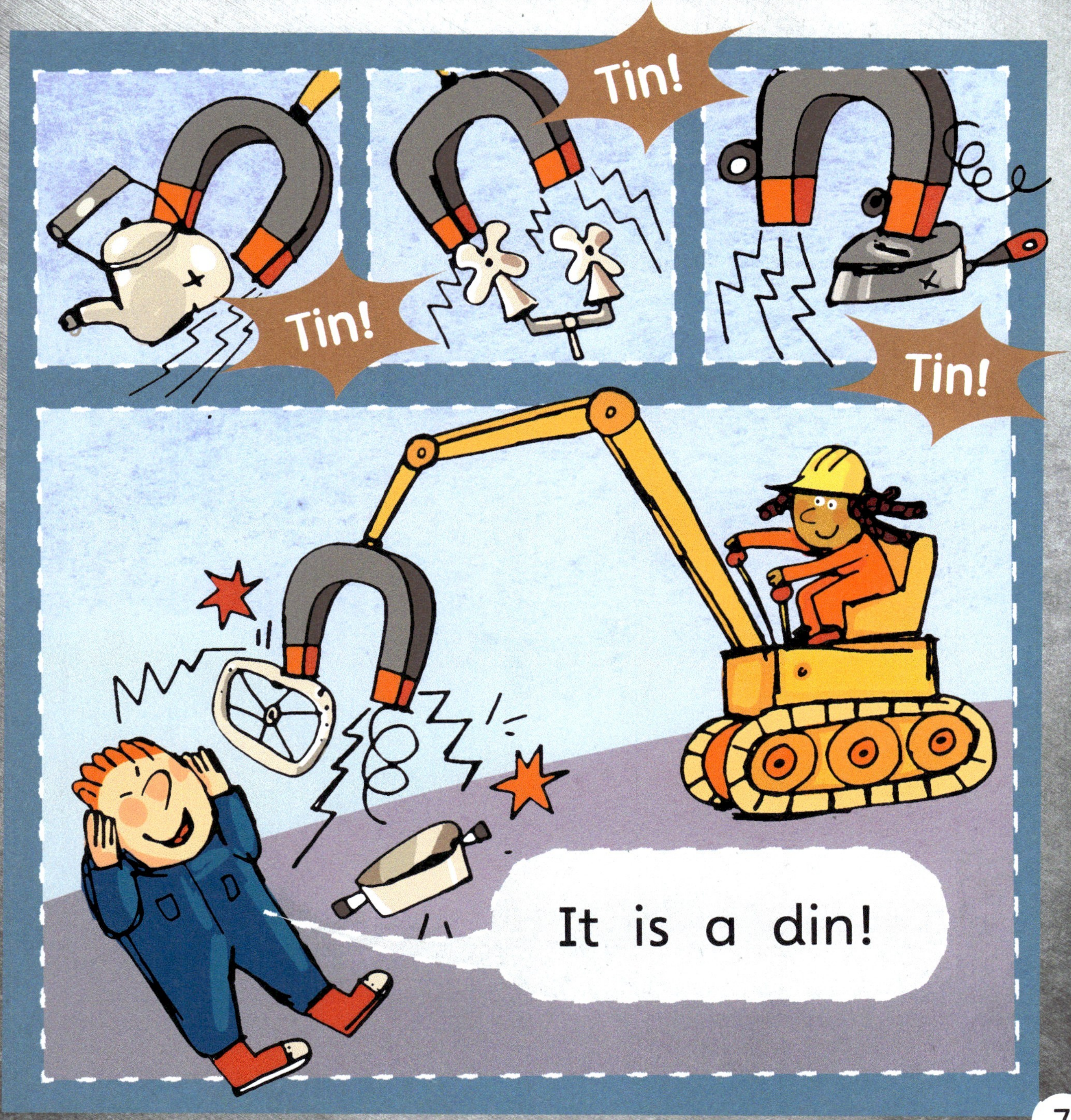
Tin!
Tin!
Tin!
It is a din!

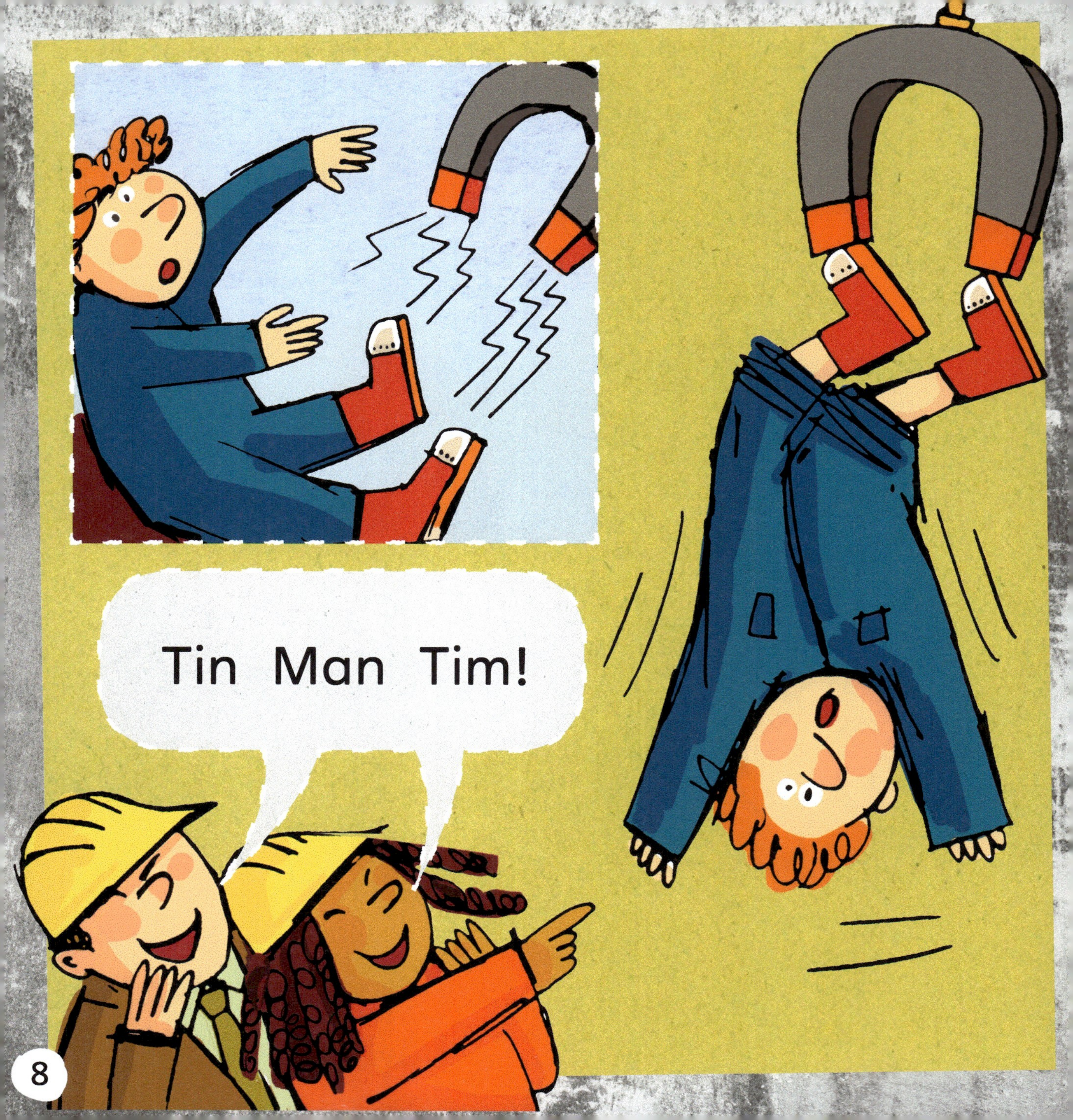
Tin Man Tim!